Imagining the Future

Community Helpers of the PAST, PRESENT, and FUTURE

Linda Bozzo

Bailey Books

an imprint of

Enslow Publishers, Inc.

40 Industrial Road

Box 398

Berkeley Heights, NJ 07922

USA

http://www.enslow.com

Bailey Books, an imprint of Enslow Publishers, Inc.

Library of Congress Cataloging-in-Publication Data

Bozzo, Linda.
    Community helpers of the past, present, and future / Linda Bozzo.
        p. cm. — (Imagining the future)
    Includes index.
    Summary: "Readers will learn about the history, present, and dream about the possible futures of different community helpers, such as doctors, teachers, firefighters, librarians, mail carriers, veterinarians, dentists, and police officers"—Provided by publisher.
    ISBN 978-0-7660-3435-8
    1. Municipal services—Juvenile literature. 2. Professions—Juvenile literature. I. Title.
HD4431.B82 2011
331.7'93—dc22

2010011594

Printed in the United States of America

062010 Lake Book Manufacturing, Inc., Melrose Park, IL

10 9 8 7 6 5 4 3 2 1

♻ Enslow Publishers, Inc., is committed to printing our books on recycled paper. The paper in every book contains 10% to 30% post-consumer waste (PCW). The cover board on the outside of each book contains 100% PCW. Our goal is to do our part to help young people and the environment too!

Illustration Credits: © Naomi Bassitt/iStockphoto.com, p. 14 (bottom); © Bonnie Jacobs/iStockphoto.com, p. 8 (bottom); Tom LaBaff, pp. 1, 7, 9, 11, 13, 15, 17, 19, 21; Library of Congress, pp. 6 (top), 10 (top), 12 (top), 16 (top), 18 (top), 22 (top); National Postal Museum, p. 14 (top); New York Public Library Archives, The New York Public Library, Astor, Lenox, and Tilden Foundations, p. 4; Photos.com, p. 20; © Yury Shirokov/iStockphoto.com, p. 18 (bottom); Shutterstock.com, pp. 3, 5, 6 (bottom), 10 (bottom), 12 (bottom), 16 (bottom), 22 (bottom); State Library and Archives of Florida, pp. 2, 8 (top).

Cover Illustrations: front cover—Tom LaBaff; back cover—Library of Congress (top inset); Shutterstock.com (bottom inset).

CONTENTS

The History of Community Helpers

Yesterday

A **community** helper is someone who helps make a neighborhood a better place. How people serve their communities has changed over the years.

Years ago, firefighters needed longer ladders to fight fires in new tall buildings. Doctors needed new **medicines** to save lives.

Today

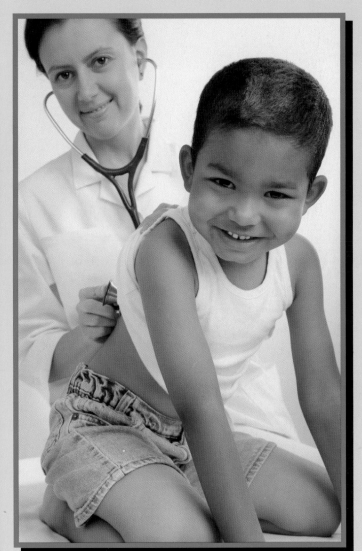

Times have changed. It takes many people to run communities today. Community helpers have new machines and tools so they can do better jobs.

Tomorrow

How do you think community helpers will do their jobs in the **future**?

1. Doctor

Yesterday

Doctors once had very few medicines to treat sick people.

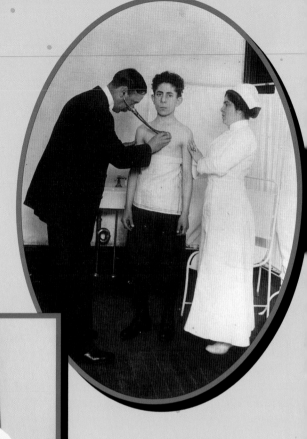

Today

Today, there are many medicines to help make sick people better.

Tomorrow

What if, many years from now, your doctor did not have an office? A big screen in your bedroom might bring the doctor right into your house. Staying home could help keep others from catching your cold.

2. Teacher

Yesterday

Teachers once taught children of all ages in one room.

Today

Now, children in each class are usually about the same age.

Maybe one day children will not be taught in classrooms. What if everyone were connected through small computers? You could read while your mother shopped. You could talk to your teacher from the car. What if you could even learn math while taking your bath? You could learn from just about anywhere!

3. Firefighter

Yesterday

Firefighters once had few tools to fight fires. Horses pulled the fire trucks.

Today

Today, firefighters use new and better tools. Fire trucks are big and powerful.

What might fire engines look like many years from now? Would firefighters still use hoses and water? Firefighters might not have to go into burning buildings. They might direct robots from outside. Firefighters' jobs would be much safer.

4. Librarian

Yesterday

Librarians did not always have computers in the **library**.

Today

Now, librarians use computers to help people.

What if the librarian of the future could turn into a character from your favorite book? Would you like her to read it to you?

5. Mail Carrier

Mail carriers once delivered mail using a horse and buggy.

Today

Today, mail trucks are often used to deliver mail. Some mail carriers walk to your house with the mail.

How will mail carriers deliver mail many years from now? They might deliver mail through your computer. Or they might drive trucks that put the mail right in your mailbox. Either way, they would not have to walk through the rain or snow to get to your house.

6. Veterinarian

Yesterday

At one time, **veterinarians** cared mostly for farm animals, like horses.

Today

Veterinarians still care for horses. They also care for pets such as cats, dogs, and birds.

Imagine if in the future the veterinarian could communicate with your pet. It would make it easier for the vet to figure out what was wrong and help your pet get well.

7. Dentist

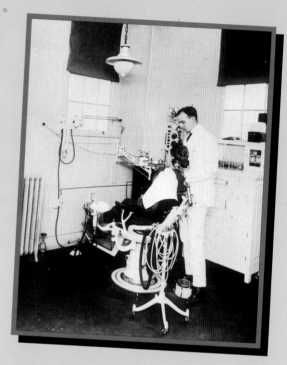

Yesterday

Dentists once had very few tools to help with tooth problems.

Today

Today, dentists have better ways to fix tooth problems and keep teeth healthy.

What if you never had to brush your teeth again? Super machines would scrub your teeth super clean during visits—so clean that you might never have to brush again! What if there were no more sugar, so it would be easier to keep teeth healthy? Dentists would have more time to go on vacation!

8. Police Officer

Yesterday

Long ago, some police officers walked on the job. Some rode horses or bicycles. They had no radios to talk to each other.

Today

Today, many police officers ride in patrol cars with lights and sirens. These cars have radios and computers.

Tomorrow

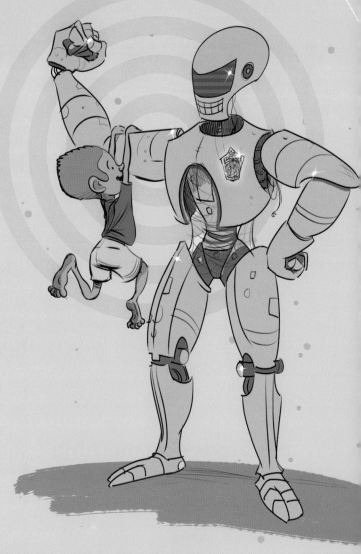

What might a police officer's job be like many years from now? Will they still be riding in patrol cars? Maybe the cars will fly. Maybe they will ride on water. Do you know what will never change? A police officer will always be your friend.

The world we live in is always changing. No one really knows what will happen in the future. We can only imagine!

WORDS TO KNOW

community—A group of people living in the same area.

future—The time after today.

library—A place where books are kept.

medicine—Something used to treat illnesses.

veterinarian—A doctor who takes care of animals.

Learn More

Books

Jango-Cohen, Judith. *Librarians*. Minneapolis: Lerner Publications, 2005.

Kalman, Bobbie. *Firefighters to the Rescue!* New York: Crabtree Publishing, 2005.

Leake, Diyan. *Dentists*. Chicago: Heinemann Library, 2008.

Rau, Dana Meachen. *Doctors*. Tarrytown, N.Y.: Marshall Cavendish Benchmark, 2008.

Web Sites

Kids at Work: Job Play—Hospital
<http://www.knowitall.org/kidswork/hospital/jobplay/index.html>

HUD: The Kids Next Door—What's My Job?
<http://www.hud.gov/kids/whatsjob.html>

INDEX